Men, Women and Children
in
Roman Britain

Jane Bingham

WAYLAND

First published in 2010 by Wayland

Copyright © Wayland 2010

Wayland
338 Euston Road
London NW1 3BH

Wayland
Level 17/207 Kent Street
Sydney, NSW 2000

British Library Cataloguing in Publication Data
Bingham, Jane
   Men, women and children in Roman Britain
   1. Great Britain--History--Roman period, 55 B.C. -449 A.D.--Juvenile literature
   2. Great Britain--Social life and customs--To 1066--Juvenile literature
   I. Title
   936.1.'04-dc22

ISBN: 978 0 7502 6232 3

Printed in China

Wayland is a division of Hachette Children's Books, an Hachette UK Company.
www.hachette.co.uk

Picture acknowledgments: AA World Travel Library/Alamy: 8; Ancient Art & Architecture Collection Ltd: Cover (BL), 5, 7, 11, 17, 22, 23, 26; Bignor Roman Villa, www.bignorromanvilla.co.uk <http://www.bignorromanvilla.co.uk/> : 25; © The Trustees of the British Museum: 19; English Heritage Photo Library: 14, 21, 24; Peter Horree/Alamy: Cover (TL), 27; © Museum of London: Cover (main), 10; G. Owston (London)/Alamy: 9; John Prior Images/Alamy: 12; Rolf Richardson/Alamy: 15; Steve Sant/Alamy: title page, 18; Neil Setchfield/Alamy: 4, 13; Shutterstock: Cover (CL); Ian Thompson 6; Nick Turner/Alamy: 20; Verulamium Museum, St Albans, Hertfordshire, UK/Bridgeman Art Library, London: 16

Contents

Words that appear in **bold** can be found in the glossary on page 28.

BRITAIN IN ROMAN TIMES

For over 350 years, Britain was part of the Roman Empire. In 43CE, a Roman army conquered southern Britain, and very soon afterwards **settlers** arrived from Rome and other parts of the empire. The Romans built towns and villas, roads and army camps. They introduced Roman laws and worshipped Roman gods. Most people in Britain soon got used to the Roman way of life. They even began to think of themselves as Romans.

WHO WERE THE ROMANS?

The Romans began as a wandering tribe in central Italy. By 300BCE they had set up a capital in Rome, and had started conquering other lands. In 27BCE, the Roman Empire was founded. Over the next century it grew rapidly, reaching its largest size in 117CE. At this time it stretched 2,500 miles from east to west, and was home to more than 50 million people. The empire lasted for 500 years, but by the year 400, tribes of **barbarians** had begun to attack its borders. In 476, Rome was invaded and the Roman Empire collapsed.

► This map of Roman Britain shows the main cities and towns.

TIMELINE OF ROMAN BRITAIN

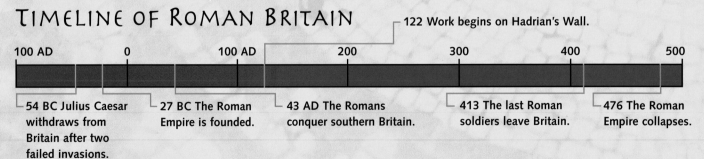

122 Work begins on Hadrian's Wall.

100 AD — 0 — 100 AD — 200 — 300 — 400 — 500

54 BC Julius Caesar withdraws from Britain after two failed invasions.

27 BC The Roman Empire is founded.

43 AD The Romans conquer southern Britain.

413 The last Roman soldiers leave Britain.

476 The Roman Empire collapses.

The Romans in Britain

The Romans tried to conquer Britain three times. Julius Caesar led two invasions, in 55 and 54BCE, but both times he withdrew his troops. Then in 43CE Emperor Claudius sent an invading army. This invasion was successful and the Romans gradually gained control of southern Britain.

The Romans ruled Britain for about 370 years. However, by the year 400, their soldiers were needed in Rome, to defend their capital from Barbarians. In 413CE the last Roman soldiers left Britain. After the army left, the British people gradually abandoned the Roman way of life.

▲ This carving shows a soldier in the invading Roman army. His horse is trampling on a British man. After the invasion, the Britons soon got used to the Roman soldiers and many Britons joined the Roman army.

Romans and Celts

Whenever the Romans tried to move into Scotland or Wales they were resisted by fierce Celtic warriors. To make matters worse for the Romans, the Scottish Celts kept attacking them. In 122CE, Emperor Hadrian gave orders for a massive wall to be built across northern England.

Hadrian's Wall was designed to keep the Celts out. It also marked the northern border of the Roman Empire.

LIFE BEFORE THE ROMANS

Before the Romans arrived, in 43CE, Britain was home to tribes of Celts. The first Celtic people lived in central Europe and gradually spread out to many parts of Europe. All the Celtic tribes spoke a similar language. They were skilled metalworkers and musicians, but they were also warlike and their tribes often fought each other.

▲ This **reconstruction** shows how a small Celtic farm would have looked. Celtic settlements were usually larger than this.

FAMILY LIFE AND RELIGION

Most British Celts lived in small **settlements**. These were groups of circular huts surrounded by a fence. Celtic men and women played the harp, and sang songs about their battle heroes.

They believed that powerful spirits lived in streams and woods. Priests called **druids** held outdoor **ceremonies** in these sacred places.

CELTIC DRESS

The Celts dressed in woollen tunics and cloaks, with colourful **plaid** designs. Men and women wore brooches, and warriors carried shields, decorated with swirling patterns. Before they went into battle, warriors smeared their bodies with blue war-paint, known as **woad**.

RESISTING THE ROMANS

Some Celtic leaders refused to be ruled by the Romans. King Caratacus fought for eight years before he was defeated in 50CE. Queen Boudicca led a revolt in 60CE. Gradually, however, the Celtic leaders came to accept Roman rule, and some of them even became local **governors**.

REAL LIVES

BOUDICCA: A CELTIC QUEEN

Boudicca was married to the ruler of the Iceni tribe in East Anglia. When her husband died, the Romans tried to seize control of her kingdom. They also stripped and flogged Queen Boudicca. This enraged Boudicca and her people. She gathered a band of warriors and marched west, attacking the Roman towns of Colchester, London and Saint Albans. All three towns were burnt to the ground before Boudicca was defeated. Some records say she poisoned herself, rather than be captured by the Romans.

Men, women and children in Roman Britain

After the Romans took control in Britain, life began to change for the British people. Under Roman law, men had more rights than they had in Celtic times. Meanwhile, British women had less freedom than before. Some poorer **Britons** lost their freedom completely and became slaves (see page 21).

Roman men

According to Roman law, men had total power over their wives and children. They were the 'master' in their home and all their orders had to be obeyed. The man of the house had a duty to take care of everyone in his household. This included his wife and children and any other relations living in the house. Wealthy men were also responsible for all the household slaves and their families.

▲ Roman men, women and children usually dressed in simple tunics and cloaks. The clothes of wealthy men were decorated with embroidery, and women wore jewellery.

Roman women

In Roman Britain, all the important jobs were taken by men. There was no place for a powerful female leader like Boudicca. Women also played no part in war. Before the Romans arrived, some Celtic women had fought alongside their men, but Roman women stayed well away from any fighting. The job of a Roman wife was to support her husband by running the family home.

ROMAN CHILDREN

Children in Roman Britain had to obey their parents at all times. Roman fathers even had the power to put a disobedient child to death – but in fact this happened only very rarely. Children from poor families were also expected to help their parents in their work.

▶ Roman parents were very strict, but they still loved their children. This carved head of a young boy comes from a Roman grave. His parents must have had it made to remind them of their dead son.

REAL LIVES

CLAUDIA: AN ARMY COMMANDER'S WIFE

Claudia Severa was the wife of an army camp commander. She lived in the 1st century in a camp close to Hadrian's Wall. We know a little about her life through a letter she sent to Sulpicia, another commander's wife. In her letter, Claudia invites Sulpicia to her birthday party, and sends greetings from her husband and her little son. The letter is in Claudia's own handwriting, showing that she was well educated. It also shows that the wives of senior soldiers had time for fun and parties.

WHO WAS IN CHARGE?

The Roman **province** of Britannia was a run by a governor. He received his orders from the emperor in Rome and reported directly back to Rome. The governor was helped in his work by two men: a legal and a financial advisor. Roman army generals and local governors also played important roles in running Roman Britain.

THE GOVERNOR

The governor of Britannia had to control the army and keep law and order. He made sure that people paid their taxes, and he planned new roads and towns. In order to be chosen as governor, a man had to be a great army general. Most of the British governors were skilled lawyers too.

ARMY GENERALS

Army generals had a very important position in Roman Britain. By the 2nd century CE, there were three generals in Britain. Each of them was responsible for a **legion** of about 5,000 men.

▼ Hadrian's Wall marked the northern border of Roman Britain. Guarding soldiers kept a constant lookout for attacks.

The generals' most important job was keeping Britain safe. They set up guards all along the borders of the province. They also ordered their soldiers to resist any Celtic attacks. In peacetime, the generals **supervised** building work. They gave orders for their men to build forts, bridges and roads.

REGIONAL CONTROL

The Romans divided Britain into regions called **civitates**. There were roughly 14 *civitates*, and each one had its own governor. The governor of a *civitas* organized the local law courts and tax collectors. He also supervised public buildings and roads. Many local governors were **native** Britons, and some of them had been kings of tribes.

REAL LIVES

AGRICOLA: A GOVERNOR OF BRITAIN

Agricola was a Roman general and governor of Britannia from 78-84CE. At that time, Celtic tribes in Wales and Scotland were fiercely resisting Roman rule. Agricola fought off Celtic attacks in Wales and northern Britain. He also managed to conquer parts of Scotland (but these lands were later lost). After Agricola's victories in Scotland, the Emperor Domitian called him back to Rome, perhaps because he was jealous of his success. Agricola ended his life as an army general in Germany.

What was life like at home in Roman Britain?

By the year 100, the Romans were building all kinds of homes in Britain. For the super-rich, there were palaces with dozens of rooms. Wealthy people divided their time between a comfortable house in town and a villa in the country. Poor families were not so lucky. Most of them had to live in tiny huts in the country or crowded flats in town.

Life in Towns

For families with money, life in a Roman town was very pleasant. They lived in a town house, known as a *domus*, which was built around a central garden. The family had special rooms for entertaining guests. Slaves cooked their food and served it on low tables, while the family lay on couches to eat.

▲ Wealthy Roman families lived in style. The floors of their country villas were covered with mosaics and the walls were decorated with marble panels. Guests could enjoy the gardens or relax on couches and be served by slaves.

Poor people in towns had a miserable life. Often a whole family was crammed into a single room in an apartment block (known as an *insula*). Most apartment rooms had no place to wash or go to the toilet and no cooking stove. People had to buy all their food from stalls on the street.

LIVING IN A VILLA

Wealthy families loved to escape from town to their country villa. Villas were large farmhouses surrounded by gardens and fields. Most villas had a set of hot and cold baths where the family and their guests could relax. There was a study where the master could work, shady gardens to enjoy in summer and under-floor heating to keep people warm in winter.

Dozens of slaves worked in a Roman villa, running the farm, cooking and cleaning, and looking after the family. Many of the

▲ The Romans invented a clever heating method, called the hypocaust system. Hot air from a furnace flowed into the spaces underneath a villa's mosaic floors and kept the whole villa warm.

slaves had no family home. Instead they slept in dormitories, with rows of beds side by side.

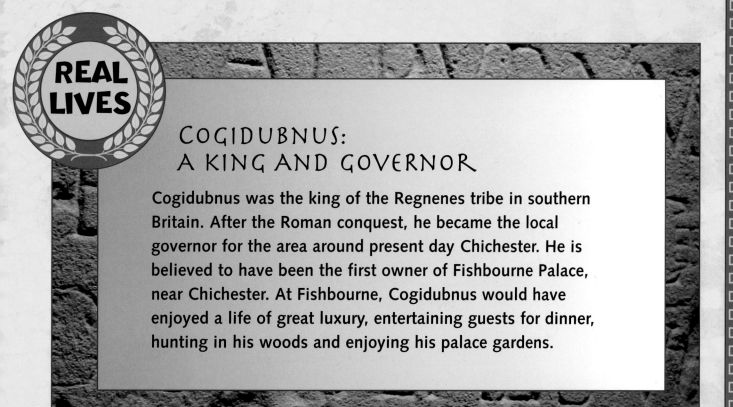

REAL LIVES

COGIDUBNUS: A KING AND GOVERNOR

Cogidubnus was the king of the Regnenes tribe in southern Britain. After the Roman conquest, he became the local governor for the area around present day Chichester. He is believed to have been the first owner of Fishbourne Palace, near Chichester. At Fishbourne, Cogidubnus would have enjoyed a life of great luxury, entertaining guests for dinner, hunting in his woods and enjoying his palace gardens.

DID CHILDREN GO TO SCHOOL?

The Romans introduced the idea of schools to Britain. Before the Roman conquest, the Celtic people did not use writing. Instead, they relied on stories and songs to teach the customs and history of their tribe. However, once the Romans took control, people had to learn to read and write - and they had to do it in Latin!

LEARNING LATIN

All over the Roman Empire, the Romans used Latin to help them run things smoothly. Latin was the language of lawyers, administrators, merchants and the army. This meant that anyone who wanted a good career had to learn Latin. The sons and daughters of the very rich were taught by a tutor at home. Boys from less wealthy families went to school, but only a very few girls were given the chance to attend.

TWO-STAGE EDUCATION

At the age of seven, pupils went to a school called a *ludus*. There they learnt the basics of reading and writing in Latin and did simple sums. They wrote on wax tablets, using a metal pen called a *stylus*.

Most pupils finished school at the age of 11, but a few went on to a secondary school, called a *grammaticus*. At the *grammaticus* boys studied literature, mathematics, history and geography. They also practised the art of public speaking.

◄ This collection of Roman writing materials includes a metal stylus and a set of wooden tablets which would have been filled with wax. There is also equipment for sealing letters with string and sealing wax, and some personal seals to stamp on the hot wax.

LEARNING AT HOME

Poor children in Roman Britain did not go to school. Instead, they helped their parents with their work. Boys learned from their fathers how to farm or work at a trade. Mothers taught their daughters how to cook and clean and look after a family. Country girls also learned to weave and sew, so they could make the family's clothes.

▼ The remains of a Roman writing tablet were found at the army camp at Vindolanda (see Real Lives panel below). The writing is some lines copied from Virgil's famous poem, the *Aeneid*.

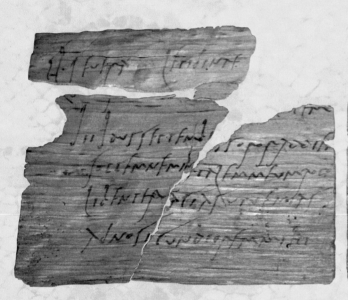

A ROMAN PUPIL

There is evidence that some Roman army commanders sent their children to school. A Roman writing tablet has been found in the ruins of the army camp at Vindolanda, close to Hadrian's Wall. Archeologists think that the tablet belonged to a school pupil, who was living with his parents in the camp.

WHAT JOBS DID PEOPLE DO?

Jobs in Roman Britain depended on a person's class and where they lived. Most poor people living in the country worked on the land. The towns were full of shopkeepers and craftworkers. Wealthy men had the top jobs in government and the army. The toughest jobs of all, such as mining, were done by slaves.

A SOLDIER'S LIFE

▲ These men are dressed as Roman soldiers. They are led by their commander, two standard-bearers and a man with a horn that is blown when fighting begins.

Young men who had a little education could join the army. Roman soldiers had to train hard for battle, but a soldier's life was not just about fighting. Members of the army also worked as engineers, cooks and builders.

Many soldiers were based in remote camps on the British borders. When they retired from the army, aged around 45, soldiers moved to retirement towns close to the camps where they had worked.

WORKING ON THE LAND

Most poor country families were employed by their local villa owner. Men, women and children worked very long hours, labouring in the fields and looking after the animals. The hardest jobs on the farm were done by slaves, who were owned by the master of the villa.

MINERS

Roman Britain was famous for its mines, which exported tin, gold, silver and lead to the other parts of the empire. But mining was hard and dangerous work. Miners worked underground in dark, cramped tunnels. Many of them died from lung disease and lead poisoning. Not surprisingly, few free men were miners. Instead, the mines were worked by slaves, who had been captured as prisoners of war.

► This small statue shows a Roman farmer working in the fields. He holds onto a plough that is pulled by oxen.

REAL LIVES

MARCUS: A SOLDIER

A tombstone found in Bath (on the site of the Roman city of Aquae Sulis) records the career of a Roman soldier. Marcus Valerius Latinus joined the army at the age of 15 and served for 20 years until his death, aged 35. He began as an ordinary soldier and rose through the ranks, becoming an *eques* (a mounted **cavalry** officer) and then a centurion (a commander in charge of around 80 men). The tombstone does not record how he died.

MERCHANTS

Trade was an important part of life in Roman Britain. British merchants sailed to distant parts of the Roman Empire, taking precious metals and wool to exchange for goods such as spices, oil, wine and silk. Merchants from overseas also came to Britain, and some of them even settled in Britannia (see Real Lives panel on page 21).

CRAFTWORKERS

Skilled craftworkers set up workshops in British towns, making a range of goods from simple pots and pans to elaborate jewellery and fine mosaics. Workshops were often run as a family business with the adults and children all working together.

APOTHECARIES AND DOCTORS

When people fell sick in Roman Britain, they usually visited an **apothecary**'s shop. Apothecaries made medicines, ointments and pills from herbs and minerals. Only the rich could afford to visit a doctor. Roman doctors tried to cure fevers by draining off some of their patients' blood. They also performed simple operations, such as **amputating** a limb with a saw. They had no **antiseptic** to put on wounds. Instead they used honey to keep wounds moist and clean.

◄ This man is dressed as a Roman doctor. He is preparing some ointment for his patients.

▲ A bronze lamp moulded in the form of a slave boy. The boy is wrapped in a cloak and sits on a stool.

SLAVES AND FREEMEN

Most slaves in Roman Britain were foreign prisoners of war, but some were native Britons. Slaves had no rights and belonged entirely to their master or mistress. Many slaves had to work incredibly hard, but some had fairly pleasant lives as household slaves. A few well-educated slaves had jobs as librarians or tutors.

Some masters granted freedom to their slaves after many years of loyal service. Freed slaves – both men and women – were known as 'freedmen'. They had the right to buy their own house and could even keep slaves of their own.

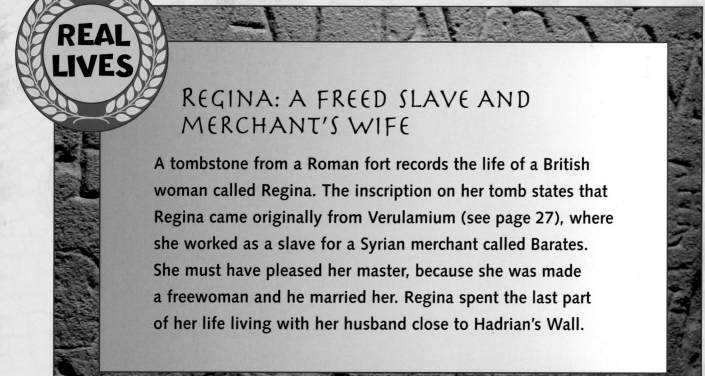

REAL LIVES

REGINA: A FREED SLAVE AND MERCHANT'S WIFE

A tombstone from a Roman fort records the life of a British woman called Regina. The inscription on her tomb states that Regina came originally from Verulamium (see page 27), where she worked as a slave for a Syrian merchant called Barates. She must have pleased her master, because she was made a freewoman and he married her. Regina spent the last part of her life living with her husband close to Hadrian's Wall.

WHAT DID PEOPLE EAT?

Before the Roman conquest, the Celts had a very limited diet. People of all classes ate a kind of porridge made from corn, plus some vegetables and berries. They had very little meat and used honey to make a sweet drink. After the Romans arrived, in 43CE, meals in Britain changed dramatically – especially for the rich.

◀ This carved scene shows a grand banquet. The guests are drinking from bowls, and being served by slaves.

NEW FOODS

Roman farmers in Britain planted a range of vegetables, including garlic, onions, cabbages and peas. They introduced new fruit, such as apples and cherries, and grew a special kind of corn which was good for making into bread. Roman landowners reared pigs and chickens for their meat and introduced new animals, such as hares and pheasants, into the British woods.

FOOD FOR THE RICH

Wealthy Romans in Britain held astonishing banquets for their guests. These feasts lasted for hours and had dozens of courses – all designed to impress. Banquets often included roast wild boar, swans, geese and ducks. They also featured smaller dishes such as dormice sprinkled with honey and poppy seeds.

Even when they weren't entertaining guests, wealthy families still ate large amounts of meat. Many of the dishes were served with a strong-tasting sauce, to disguise the fact that the meat was not always very fresh!

SOLDIERS' MEALS

Soldiers ate a lot of porridge and stew. They munched through large amounts of bread, which was baked in huge ovens in the army camps. Bacon was also very popular. Each group of eight soldiers carried a folding frying pan, so they could fry up their bacon when they were on the march.

▲ Roman cooks used very simple equipment. This reconstruction of a Roman kitchen shows a copper cooking pot standing on an iron grill above some heated coals.

REAL LIVES

A ROMAN STOREKEEPER

A storekeeper's records have been found on the site of the army camp at Vindolanda. They show that he was kept very busy ordering food, including special treats, such as wild boar, for the camp's commanding officer. One shopping list shows the large quantities he had to order. It includes twenty chickens, a hundred apples and two hundred eggs.

HOW DID ADULTS AND CHILDREN HAVE FUN?

Life was not all work in Roman Britain, and people of all classes found time to have fun. Men, women and children enjoyed sports and indoor games. They also took advantage of the various public entertainments provided in the towns.

▲ This Roman game has a stone 'board' marked out with squares and red and white counters made from pottery.

SPORTS AND GAMES

Wealthy men and boys went hunting for birds and wild animals, and practised wrestling, running and boxing. Poor men also held wrestling matches and played a range of ball games, including an early version of hockey. Children played with rag dolls and wooden swords and bowled hoops along the ground. Some wealthy boys and girls had miniature carts that were pulled by goats or ponies. Men, women and children enjoyed playing board games.

PUBLIC ENTERTAINMENTS

People living in towns could visit the theatre to see a comedy, a tragedy, or a comic mime. They could watch chariot racers hurtle down a track. Or they could visit the local **amphitheatre**: a large stone stadium, with rows of seats rising up on all sides.

◄ This mosaic from a Roman villa in Bignor, West Sussex, shows two gladiators fighting each other.

Amphitheatres were used for public executions, for fights between wild beasts, and for gladiator battles. Gladiators were trained to fight in one-to-one combat until one of them died.

ROMAN BATHS

Most Roman towns had a set of public baths. These included a hot bath, a warm bath, and a cold **plunge**. There was also a steam room, a massage room, and an exercise yard. The baths were open to all adults except slaves.

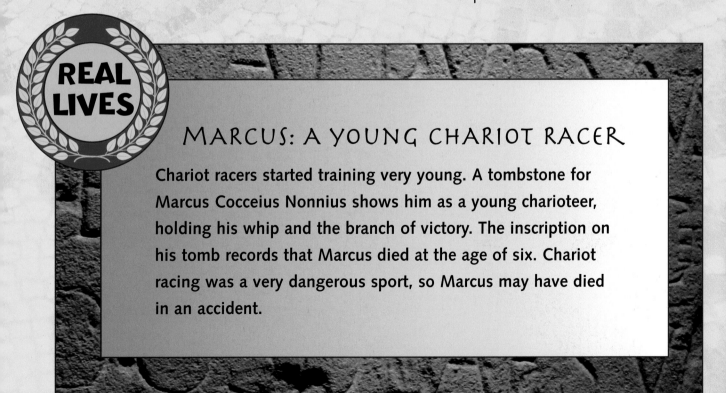

REAL LIVES

MARCUS: A YOUNG CHARIOT RACER

Chariot racers started training very young. A tombstone for Marcus Cocceius Nonnius shows him as a young charioteer, holding his whip and the branch of victory. The inscription on his tomb records that Marcus died at the age of six. Chariot racing was a very dangerous sport, so Marcus may have died in an accident.

HOW IMPORTANT WAS RELIGION IN ROMAN BRITAIN?

After the Roman conquest, the Romans introduced their religion to Britain, but people did not only worship Roman gods. Some British people continued to believe in Celtic nature spirits, and the new religion of Christianity grew rapidly.

▲ Venus, the Roman goddess of love and beauty, is shown in this mosaic.

ROMAN GODS

The Romans worshipped a large number of gods and goddesses, including Jupiter, the ruler of the gods, Mars, the god of the war, and Minerva, the goddess of wisdom. Even the Roman emperors were worshipped as gods.

All over Britain, temples were built in honour of the gods, and public ceremonies were held. Everyone had to attend these ceremonies, to show their respect for the Romans and their gods.

NATURE SPIRITS

When the Romans first arrived in Britain, they saw the druids (Celtic priests) as their enemies. However, the Roman governors soon became more relaxed about the Celts' beliefs. In Roman Britain, people still visited their ancient sacred places, and some worshipped Celtic spirits combined with Roman gods.

THE COMING OF CHRISTIANITY

By the year 200, the Christian faith was spreading fast through Britain. However, it was dangerous to be an early Christian. Christians refused to worship the Roman gods, including the emperor, and this was seen as a crime that should be punished by death. Many of the first Christians in Britain were beheaded.

In 313, Christianity was made the official religion of the Roman Empire, and the **persecution** of Christians came to an end. Christians in Britain began to meet in small chapels, which were sometimes decorated with paintings and carvings.

▲ The goddess Sulis Minerva was worshipped in Aqua Sulis (present-day Bath).

REAL LIVES

ALBAN: A CHRISTIAN SOLDIER

Alban was a soldier in the city of Verulamium in the 3rd century. Even though he worshipped the Roman gods, he decided to help a Christian priest, who was escaping from persecution. Alban hid the priest in his house and very soon became a Christian too. When the hiding place was discovered, Alban was arrested and given a trial. He refused to give up his Christian faith, so he was beheaded. Later, he was recognized as a Christian saint, and the town of Verulamium was given the name 'Saint Albans'.

Glossary

administrators People who run an organization or part of a country.

amphitheatre A large public building in which entertainments such as gladiator contests were held.

amputate Cut off.

antiseptic A substance that kills germs.

apothecary Someone like a chemist who prepares medicines, pills and ointments.

barbarians The name the Romans gave to the tribes who lived outside the Roman Empire.

Britons People who were living in Britain when the Romans invaded.

cavalry Soldiers who ride into battle on horseback.

ceremonies Special religious events or services.

charioteer A chariot racer.

civitas (plural **civitates**) an area of Roman Britain, rather like a county.

druids Celtic priests.

gladiator Someone who was forced to fight as a public entertainment. Gladiators were usually slaves or prisoners of war.

governor Someone who ran a country or large area within the Roman Empire.

legion A large group of soldiers. Legions contained around 5,000 men.

native Belonging to a country.

persecution Very cruel treatment of people, often because of their religion.

plaid A pattern of large checks, used in Scottish kilts.

plunge A very cold pool that you dip into quickly.

province A region of the Roman Empire, such as Britannia (Britain) that had its own governor.

reconstruction An imitation of something from the past, such as a Celtic village, or a Roman doctor's surgery.

settlements Places where a group of people live together.

settlers People who arrive in a place and decide to make their home there.

supervise to check that work is done correctly.

woad A type of blue war-paint that Celtic warriors used to smear on their bodies before battle to make themselves look frightening.

FURTHER INFORMATION

MORE BOOKS TO READ

Jane Bingham
Men, Women and Children in Ancient Rome
(Wayland, 2009)

Ruth Brocklehurst
Roman Britain
(Usborne, 2008)

Tim Locke
Britain in Roman Times
(Franklin Watts, 2008)

Jillian Powell
The Gruesome Truth About the Romans
(Wayland, 2008)

Philip Steele
100 Things you should know about Roman Britain
(Miles Kelly, 2004)

Rosemary Sutcliff
Eagle of the Ninth
(Oxford University Press, 2004)
(An exciting novel about a Roman centurion in Britain)

USEFUL WEBSITES

http://www.roman-empire.net/
A massive site on Roman history and culture. Includes a Kids' Section.

http://www.bbc.co.uk/schools/romans/
A lively website, organized by topics such as the Roman army, leisure, and family and children. It includes activities and fun facts.

http://www.salariya.com/web_books/gladiator/index.html
A humorous view of the life of a Roman gladiator.

http://gwydir.demon.co.uk/jo/games/romgame/index.htm
A site devoted to Roman games.

PLACES TO VISIT

The Roman baths at Bath, Somerset
http://www.romanbaths.co.uk/

Chedworth Roman Villa, Gloucestershire
http://www.chedworthromanvilla.com/

Fishbourne Roman Palace, Sussex
http://www.sussexpast.co.uk/property/site.php?site_id=11

Lullingstone Roman Villa, Kent
http://www.english-heritage.org.uk/server/show/nav.14714

Roman Army Museum at Vindolanda, Northumberland
http://www.vindolanda.com/

Roman Legion Museum at Caerleon, Gwent
http://www.museumwales.ac.uk/en/roman/

INDEX

Numbers in **bold** indicate pictures.